THE AUTHENTIC YOU

The Authentic You

---

*Unlocking Your True
Potential and Living Your
Best Life*

B. VINCENT

QuantumQuill Press

CONTENTS

First Printing, 2024

Introduction: Embracing Authenticity

The Pith of Genuineness

In the embroidery of human life, genuineness remains as a reference point of truth, directing us toward an existence of profundity and importance. It is the specialty of being consistent with oneself, of adjusting one's activities, contemplations, and sentiments with one's center character and values. This arrangement, this amicability between the internal identity and the external articulation, characterizes the embodiment of credibility.

What difference does legitimacy make? The response lies in its significant effect on our prosperity and the nature of our lives. Living legitimately brings a feeling of harmony and fulfillment that is challenging to track down through some other means. It is the foundation of real satisfaction, the sort that isn't reliant upon outside conditions however moves from the profundities of our being. At the point when we live legitimately, we are on top of our real essence, and each part of our lives resounds with this reality. This concordance brings about superior emotional wellness, as the contention between what our identity is and who we claim to be scatters, decreasing pressure and tension. It cultivates more grounded, more significant connections, as we interface with others on a more profound level, unhampered by exteriors or misrepresentations. Besides, credibility enables us to lead a seriously satisfying life, loaded up with exercises and pursuits that genuinely resound with our deepest longings and values.

However, the excursion toward validness isn't without its difficulties. It expects mental fortitude to confront ourselves, to recognize our defects and weaknesses, and to embrace them as a feature of our remarkable personality. It requests strength to endure the strain to adjust to cultural assumptions that may not line up with our actual selves. In any case, the prizes of such an excursion are unlimited. To live really is to live openly, unburdened by the heaviness of misrepresentation or the apprehension about judgment. It is to explore existence with a compass that focuses resolutely toward our actual north.

As we set out on this investigation of credibility, let us recollect that it's anything but an objective however an approach to being, a consistent course of adjusting our outer life to our inward truth. The substance of realness lies not in flawlessness but rather in that frame of mind, in having every one of the responses yet in looking for them with an open heart and brain. In the pages that follow, we will dive further into this idea, uncovering the layers and aspects of living legitimately. Together, we will find how to strip back the layers of assumptions and suspicions that have clouded our actual selves, and how to step into the illumination of realness, where our actual potential is standing by.

The Job of Mindfulness

At the core of bona fide living beats the beat of mindfulness. It is the foundation whereupon the structure of genuineness is assembled, the focal point through which we can see our actual selves in the midst of the mayhem of day to day existence. Mindfulness is the cozy comprehension of our viewpoints, feelings, inspirations, and values. The mirror mirrors our most profound longings, fears, qualities, and shortcomings. This significant understanding into our inward operations is pivotal for leaving on the way to legitimacy.

For what reason is mindfulness so crucial? Since without it, we explore the waters of existence without a compass. We become powerless to the flows of cultural assumptions, social standards, and outer tensions, failing to focus on our actual course. Without mindfulness, our decisions might reflect what others need for us, instead of what we need for ourselves. It is simply by developing a profound comprehension of who we are that we can settle on choices that reverberate with our bona fide selves.

The excursion to mindfulness starts with reflection. It includes posing ourselves troublesome inquiries and being available to anything that answers might emerge, agreeable or not. It expects us to stop and consider our encounters, to distinguish the minutes when we felt most alive and those when we felt disengaged from our embodiment. Through this interaction, we start to recognize the examples of our viewpoints and ways of behaving, the hidden convictions that drive our activities, and the qualities that give our lives meaning.

Besides, mindfulness is definitely not a static accomplishment however a powerful interaction. It advances as we develop and change, adjusting to new bits of knowledge and valuable encounters. It requests persistent consideration and interest in ourselves, an eagerness to investigate the profundities of our being. This investigation isn't simple 100% of the time. Standing up to parts of ourselves that we have overlooked or suppressed can be awkward. However, it is through this uneasiness that development happens, and realness prospers.

Developing mindfulness is likened to tending a nursery. It requires tolerance, care, and ordinary sustaining. The devices of this development are fluctuated — journaling, contemplation, criticism from confided in others, and care rehearses are only a couple of techniques that can assist us with adjusting to our internal identities. As we become more receptive to our internal world, we foster the clearness and conviction to live legitimately, pursuing decisions that line up with our actual selves.

As we set out on this excursion together, recall that the way to mindfulness is both testing and fulfilling. A journey of disclosure uncovers the extravagance of our inward scene, uncovering the magnificence and intricacy of our real selves. Allow us to embrace this excursion with an open heart, for it is through mindfulness that we open the way to an existence of realness.

Outline of the Excursion

As we stand at the edge of this investigation into credibility, it means a lot to outline the landscape ahead. This book is planned as an aide, a friend on your excursion to revealing and living your actual self. The parts that follow are venturing stones, every one taking you more profound into the core of credibility, from the genuinely trustworthy, underlying arousing of mindfulness to the development of true connections and the route of the computerized world.

This excursion isn't straight; it reflects the intricacies and subtleties of life itself. It winds through the inward scenes of self-revelation, over the obstacles of cultural assumptions, and into the ripe grounds of certifiable self-articulation. Every part expands upon the last, making a thorough pathway towards carrying on with a day to day existence that is really your own.

1. Discovering Your Actual Self: We start by digging into the substance of what your identity is. This investigation is the groundwork of credibility, welcoming you to ponder your biography, distinguish your guiding principle and convictions, and perceive your interests and assets. It's tied in with stripping back the layers of outside impacts to uncover the dynamic center of your being.

2. Overcoming Hindrances to Genuineness: The way to living legitimately is frequently impeded by fears, cultural tensions, and struggles under the surface. This basic area tends to these difficulties head-on, offering systems for conquering them. It's tied in with building the mental fortitude to confront your feelings of trepidation, the solidarity to stand firm against outside pressures, and the strength to embrace your actual self, defects what not.

3. Cultivating Mindfulness: A profound plunge into the practices that upgrade self-information and understanding. This section is your manual for fostering a sharp identity mindfulness through care, journaling, and reflection. It's tied in with tuning into your inward voice and paying attention to the insights it talks.

4. Setting Genuine Objectives: Realness reaches out into the fantasies we seek after and the objectives we set for ourselves. This segment centers around adjusting your yearnings to your actual self, guaranteeing that your interests mirror your most profound qualities and wants. About making a daily existence feels better within as it maybe looks outwardly.

5. Building Legitimate Connections: Validness doesn't exist in segregation; it flourishes in the association with others. This section investigates how to frame and sustain connections that honor your actual self and regard the realness of everyone around you. About developing associations are established in weakness, trustworthiness, and shared regard.

6. Living Legitimately in a Computerized World: In our undeniably computerized age, keeping up with realness online presents special difficulties. This segment offers experiences into exploring web-based entertainment and the computerized scene without failing to focus on your actual self. It's tied in with finding equilibrium and honesty by they way you present and articulate your thoughts on the web.

As you set out on this excursion, recall that the way to validness is however extraordinary as you seem to be. There will be epiphanies and times of uncertainty, seasons of euphoria, and seasons of challenge. However, every step you make is a stride towards a more true, satisfying life. This book is here to direct you, to move you, and to help you as you find and embrace "The True You."

Normal Difficulties to Living Really

The way to validness is thronw with hindrances, each introducing its own test to our healthy identity and our assurance to honestly live. Perceiving these obstructions is the most important phase in conquering them, making ready for a day to day existence lived as one with our actual selves. This excursion, however loaded with difficulties, is profoundly fulfilling, driving us to a position of self-acknowledgment and certifiable bliss. Allow us to investigate a portion of the normal difficulties you might experience on your way to credibility.

Apprehension about Judgment: Perhaps of the most impressive hindrance on the way to realness is the feeling of dread toward how others will see us. The anxiety that our actual selves probably won't be acknowledged or appreciated can lead us to veil our genuine characters, taking on personas that we accept will be more agreeable to the world.

This segment digs into the foundations of this trepidation and offers systems for defeating it, stressing the significance of esteeming our self-esteem over outer approval.

The Snare of Correlation: In a world that continually barrages us with messages about what we ought to be, do, and have, it's not difficult to fall into the snare of examination. This challenge subverts our validness by moving our concentration from our special process to a race against others. Here, we examine how to perceive this snare and getaway it, cultivating an outlook of personal development that commends our singular advancement instead of contrasting it with that of others.

Relinquishing Hairsplitting: The quest for flawlessness can be a significant boundary to living really. This tenacious mission frequently leads us from our actual selves, as we endeavor to fulfill incomprehensible guidelines set without anyone else or society. This segment investigates the risks of hairsplitting and gives direction on embracing blemish as a characteristic and important piece of the human experience, permitting us to live more unreservedly and genuinely.

Managing Outside Tensions: The assumptions and tensions from family, society, and culture can essentially impede our capacity to legitimately live. Whether it's vocation decisions, way of life choices, or even private convictions, outer tensions can constrain us to adjust to a shape that doesn't accommodate our actual selves. We talk about how to recognize these tensions and techniques for affirming your own way, in any event, when it wanders from the assumptions for other people.

Self-Uncertainty and Instability: Maybe the most inward of obstructions, self-uncertainty, and frailty can dissolve our feeling of realness from the inside. These sentiments can make us question our value, our decisions, and our entitlement to really live. This part tends to the significance of building fearlessness and versatility, offering apparatuses for reinforcing our confidence in ourselves and our capacity to lead experiences that are consistent with our deepest selves.

Every one of these difficulties addresses an obstacle on the way to legitimacy, yet in addition a chance for development. By facing and conquering these impediments, we draw nearer to our actual selves as well as foster a more profound comprehension and sympathy for the excursion of others. The most common way of beating these obstructions is basic to the excursion of credibility, showing us versatility, mental fortitude, and the benefit of remaining consistent with ourselves in a world that frequently empowers similarity. As we explore these difficulties, we prepare for an existence of genuineness, set apart by a significant feeling of satisfaction and internal harmony.

The Commitment of Real Living

In the calm snapshots of reflection, when we strip away the layers of assumptions and cultural standards, we find at our center the commitment of credible living. A commitment murmurs of opportunity, satisfaction, and the significant delight of being consistent with oneself. Embracing genuineness isn't just a demonstration of self-revelation; it is a guarantee to explore life's intricacies with respectability and mental fortitude. This last point in our presentation enlightens the groundbreaking force of living legitimately, a signal that guides us toward our actual potential and the most ideal variant of our lives.

The Freedom of Legitimacy: There is an unrivaled freedom that accompanies living genuinely, a delivery from the imperatives of misrepresentation and the opportunity to communicate our actual selves. This segment digs into the feeling of freedom that goes with genuineness, featuring how this opportunity advances each part of our lives, from our connections to our professions, empowering us to lead experiences that are consistent with ourselves as well as profoundly fulfilling.

The Satisfaction of Being Consistent with Oneself: At the core of real living is a significant feeling of satisfaction. At the point when our activities, decisions, and communications are together as one with our actual selves, we experience life all the more completely and with more prominent fulfillment. Here, we investigate the profound satisfaction that comes from adjusting our lives to our qualities and wants, exhibiting how legitimacy goes about as a vital aspect for opening an existence of happiness and delight.

The Strength of Weakness: Legitimacy requires weakness, the boldness to appear and be recognized the truth about. This segment tends to the strength that comes from embracing our weaknesses, revealing insight into how this transparency encourages further associations with others and develops a versatile identity. It's in our eagerness to be weak that we track down our most prominent strength and the ability to associate genuinely with our general surroundings.

The Expanding influence of Realness: Living legitimately changes our own lives as well as significantly affects everyone around us. By being consistent with ourselves, we motivate others to set out on their own excursions of self-disclosure and genuineness. This part investigates the far reaching influence of genuineness, showing how our own obligation to living legitimately can impact our networks, making a flood of positive change that urges others to experience their reality.

The Excursion Ahead: As we close this presentation, we stand at the cliff of an interesting excursion — an excursion toward the legitimate self. This last direct fills in as a greeting toward embrace the experience that lies ahead, consoling perusers that while the way might be testing, the compensations of living truly are endless. Together, we will investigate the profundities of our being, stand up to the hindrances to validness, and arise engaged to carry on with our lives with reason, energy, and significant realness.

The commitment of legitimate living isn't simply an idea to hope for; it is an unmistakable, feasible condition of being that enhances each snapshot of our reality. As we leave on this excursion together, let us cling tightly to the commitment that realness offers — an existence of opportunity, satisfaction, and genuine joy. Allow the excursion to start.

| 1 |

Chapter 1: Discovering Your True Self

Thinking about Your Biography

Our excursion towards realness starts with a regressive look, a profound and intelligent investigate the mosaic of encounters that make our biography. Every one of us conveys a novel story, an embroidery woven from snapshots of euphoria, torment, win, and battle. These accounts, but shifted, act as the bedrock of our character, forming our insights, values, and convictions. To set out on the way of finding your actual self, we should initially turn the pages of our past, returning to the sections that have characterized us.

Considering your biography isn't only a practice in sentimentality; it is a demonstration of boldness. It expects us to confront our encounters with genuineness and receptiveness, to recognize our triumphs as well as our injuries. This thoughtfulness is the most vital move towards validness, for it is exclusively by understanding where we have been that we can plainly see where we really want to go.

Start by returning to the vital turning points of your life. These are the intersection, the urgent places where a choice, an occasion, or a collaboration fundamentally modified your direction. Consider individuals who have contacted your life, making permanent imprints on your personality and perspective. Think about the examples gained from both achievement and disappointment, perceiving how they have added to your development and flexibility.

As you dive into your past, move toward your recollections with consideration and sympathy. Recall that the objective isn't to pass judgment on your encounters however to grasp them. Every section of your life, whether loaded up with light or shadow, plays had an impact in forming the individual you are today. Embrace these accounts, for they hold the keys to opening your valid self.

Journaling can be an integral asset in this cycle, giving a material on which to paint the locations of your past. Compose unreservedly and without restriction, permitting your considerations and recollections to stream onto the page. Through composition, you might uncover stowed away bits of knowledge about yourself, uncovering examples and topics that have woven through your life.

This intelligent excursion is both individual and significant. It might bring out a range of feelings, from satisfaction and appreciation to torment and lament. Permit yourself to feel these feelings completely, for they are important for your human experience. It is through embracing our whole story, with every one of its intricacies and logical inconsistencies, that we can start to truly fashion a way towards living.

As you ponder your biography, recollect that you are the creator of your account. While the past has molded you, the pen for composing your future remaining parts in your grasp. This investigation is the establishment whereupon you can construct a day to day existence that genuinely reflects what your identity is, a daily existence resided with reason, energy, and credibility.

Values and Convictions: The Compass of Realness

In the journey to find our actual selves, the investigation of our qualities and convictions fills in as a directing compass. These profoundly held standards are the stars by which we explore the immense oceans of life, directing our choices, molding our ways of behaving, and characterizing a big motivator for we. Uncovering and understanding these guiding principle and convictions is a basic step towards living genuinely, for they are the substance of our personality, the bedrock whereupon our actual selves are fabricated.

Values and convictions are not acquired curios; they are picked convictions, formed by our encounters and reflections on our general surroundings. They answer the key inquiries of what we track down significant and deserving of our energy and responsibility. To live legitimately, we should initially distinguish these core values, for they enlighten the way to a daily existence that reverberates with our most profound selves.

Start this investigation by asking yourself what makes the biggest difference to you. Consider the minutes when you felt most satisfied or shocked, as these feelings frequently feature the qualities and convictions that lie at the core of your responses. Could it be said that you are driven by a mission for equity, an affection for opportunity, a promise to graciousness, or a quest for inventiveness? These are signs to the qualities that oversee your life.

Reflect, as well, on the convictions that shape your perspective on the world and your place inside it. Convictions about potential, achievement, connections, and ethical quality impact how we communicate with our world and the decisions. It's critical to recognize convictions that really mirror your comprehension and those that have been forced by others. Realness expects us to fundamentally look at and, if important, rethink these convictions to line up with our actual selves.

Journaling can again be a significant device in this cycle, giving a space to verbalize and look at your qualities and convictions. Expound on the standards you hold dear, the convictions that characterize your perspective, and the manners by which these convictions manifest in your day to day existence. Through this thoughtful interaction, you will start to see a more clear image of the qualities and convictions that really address you.

Understanding your qualities and convictions is a continuous excursion, not an objective. As you develop and change, so too may your convictions. The key is to stay open to this advancement, permitting your genuine self to arise and reappear after some time. This ease is definitely not an indication of shortcoming however a demonstration of the profundity of your obligation to living truly.

Outfitted with the information on your qualities and convictions, you are better prepared to settle on decisions that reverberate with your actual self. This arrangement is the core of credible living, making a day to day existence that isn't just satisfying yet in addition a genuine impression of what your identity is. As you push ahead on your excursion, let your qualities and convictions light the way, directing you toward an existence of realness and reason.

Interests and Interests: The Fuel for Your Genuine Excursion

Finding and embracing your interests and interests is similar to revealing the fuel that pushes you forward on your excursion towards genuineness. These are the exercises, thoughts, and pursuits that touch off your soul, invigorate your being, and give significant pleasure and satisfaction into your life. Recognizing what you are genuinely energetic about is a crucial stage in understanding your credible self, as our interests frequently mirror our most profound longings and center character.

The Disclosure of Energy: To start, consider the minutes when you feel generally invigorated and locked in. What exercises would you say you are doing? What subjects would you say you are examining? Which undertakings do you view as retaining, to the place where time appears to stop? These are your hints, the breadcrumbs driving you to your interests. It very well may be craftsmanship, science, civil rights, business venture, or in the middle between. Your interests are your own, as one of a kind as your unique mark, and they hold the way to understanding what really matters to you.

Interests as a Mirror: Your inclinations, while in some cases short lived or developing, act as a mirror reflecting parts of your character and internal world. They offer knowledge into what spellbinds your interest and drives your craving to investigate, learn, and develop. Whether a side interest's been with you since adolescence or a newly discovered interest, each interest adds to the mosaic of your legitimate self.

The Job of Interest: Interest is the compass that guides you towards your interests and interests. It urges you to investigate past your usual range of familiarity, to clarify some things, and to look for replies. Embracing interest implies permitting yourself the opportunity to follow these interests, to investigate without judgment, and to be available to where they could lead you. This investigation isn't just about finding what you love yet additionally about understanding the reason why it impacts you on a profound level.

Coordinating Interests into Life: When distinguished, the test and opportunity lie in meshing these interests and interests into the texture of your everyday existence. This incorporation revives your reality, changing daily practice into something significant and lined up with your valid self. It's tied in with tracking down ways, of all shapes and sizes, to draw in with your interests routinely, making them leisure activities as well as necessary pieces of your life's account.

The Advancement of Interests: It's vital to perceive that interests and interests can develop over the long run. What invigorates you today may not hold a similar charm tomorrow, and that is totally OK. This development is a characteristic piece of development and self-disclosure. The key is to stay open to new encounters and to keep sustaining your interest. Thusly, you guarantee that your life stays dynamic, satisfying, and really yours.

In embracing your interests and interests, you fuel your excursion towards an existence of realness. They are not simple interruptions but rather fundamental parts of what your identity is. By getting it and incorporating your interests into your life, you honor your actual self, making a day to day existence that isn't just significant yet additionally profoundly fulfilling.

Qualities and Shortcomings: Embracing Your Entire Self

In the scene of our credible selves, our assets and shortcomings structure the forms and profundities that give it shape and character. Understanding and embracing both is fundamental for exploring the way to realness. Our assets are the bedrock whereupon we can fabricate a day to day existence that lines up with our actual selves as well as permits us to contribute genuinely to our general surroundings. On the other hand, recognizing our shortcomings isn't a confirmation of rout yet a statement of our mankind and a stage toward development and personal growth.

Distinguishing Your Assets: Finding your assets includes an intelligent and genuine evaluation of what you normally succeed at. These are the characteristics, abilities, and gifts that come easily to you, the regions where you can possibly sparkle. Ponder the commendations you frequently get or the errands others look for your assistance with; these can be signs of your inborn assets. It's tied in with perceiving the worth you bring and the manners by which you have a beneficial outcome.

Recognizing Your Shortcomings: Similarly significant is the affirmation of your shortcomings. These are not blemishes to be embarrassed about however open doors for development and learning. By recognizing regions where you battle, you make the way for personal growth and self-awareness. Move toward this cycle with consideration and self-sympathy, understanding that flawlessness is a deception and that each individual has their own arrangement of difficulties to survive.

The Force of Self-Acknowledgment: At the core of this investigation is the force of self-acknowledgment. Embracing your assets and shortcomings permits you to see yourself all the more obviously and to see the value in the intricacy of your personality. This acknowledgment is definitely not a detached renunciation however a functioning hug of your entire self, with every one of its complexities and inconsistencies. It's tied in with cherishing yourself for who you are while additionally endeavoring to develop and advance.

Utilizing Qualities and Tending to Shortcomings: With an unmistakable comprehension of your assets and shortcomings, you can start to decisively use your assets while tending to your shortcomings. Utilize your assets to seek after open doors and to make significant commitments, permitting them to direct you toward living up to your true capacity. All the while, foster systems to develop or relieve your shortcomings, whether through instruction, practice, or looking for help where required.

The Job of Input: Criticism from confided in companions, family, and partners can give significant experiences into your assets and shortcomings. It offers an outer point of view that can assist with approving your self-appraisal or feature regions you might have disregarded. Embrace this criticism with a receptive outlook, seeing it as a gift that can support your excursion of self-disclosure and development.

Understanding and embracing your assets and shortcomings is a basic move toward living legitimately. It empowers you to explore existence with certainty and reason, settling on decisions that line up with your actual abilities and yearnings. By tolerating and cherishing your entire self, you make ready for a daily existence loaded up with development, satisfaction, and genuineness.

Your Credible Self-Idea: The Finish of Self-Disclosure

At the zenith of our excursion through the scenes of self-revelation, we show up at a crucial objective: the development of a legitimate self-idea. This self-idea is certainly not a static picture yet a dynamic, living articulation of who we are at our center. It incorporates our biography, values, interests, qualities, and shortcomings into a cognizant story that guides us toward living genuinely. Understanding and embracing this real self-idea is fundamental for exploring existence with reason, certainty, and honesty.

Coordinating Your Disclosures: The most common way of framing your genuine self-idea starts with the joining of your revelations. It includes winding around together the strings of your biography, the qualities and convictions that guide you, the interests that stimulate you, and the qualities and shortcomings that characterize your human experience. This embroidery of mindfulness gives an establishment whereupon your genuine self can stand solidly.

Self-Idea as Your Inward Compass: Your bona fide self-idea fills in as your inward compass, offering course and direction as you explore the intricacies of life. It assists you with settling on choices that line up with your actual self, avoid ways that don't resound with your center personality, and seek after objectives that satisfy your most profound goals. When confronted with decisions, ask yourself which choice best lines up with your legitimate self-idea, and let this guide your means.

The Smoothness of Self-Idea: Perceiving the ease of your self-concept is significant. As you develop and advance, so too will how you might interpret yourself. This development is a characteristic and sound piece of the excursion toward credibility. Embrace the changes, realizing that every emphasis of your self-idea carries you nearer to the fullest articulation of your actual self.

Living Really: Living as per your genuine self-idea implies embracing your special character and communicating it in all parts of your life. It's tied in with being consistent with yourself in your connections, vocation, leisure activities, and self-improvement. This coinciding between your internal identity and external life is the quintessence of realness, prompting a feeling of concordance, fulfillment, and happiness.

The Boldness to Be You: Embracing your valid self-idea requires fortitude. It implies standing firm in your character, in any event, when it challenges cultural standards or assumptions. It's tied in with possessing your story, values, interests, qualities, and shortcomings with satisfaction and certainty. Keep in mind, the most significant regard and cherish you can give yourself is the opportunity to be truly you.

As we finish up this part on finding your actual self, think about the excursion you've attempted. The way to understanding and embracing your genuine self-idea is both testing and profoundly fulfilling. It offers a day to day existence lived with reason, energy, and genuineness. Convey forward the experiences and information you've acquired, and let them light your direction as you keep on investigating, develop, and live really. This isn't the end however the start of a long lasting excursion of being consistent with the main individual in your life: you.

| 2 |

Chapter 2: Overcoming Barriers to Authenticity

Anxiety toward Judgment: Embracing Your True Self

The anxiety toward judgment is a considerable obstruction that a large number of us face on our way to living genuinely. It's the trepidation that our actual selves, when uncovered, won't meet the endorsement of others — family, companions, associates, or society at large. This dread can be deadening, driving us to cover our certified considerations, sentiments, and wants for a persona we consider more OK. Defeating this dread is fundamental for anybody trying to carry on with an existence of validness, a daily existence where we are consistent with ourselves in each viewpoint.

Grasping the Trepidation: At its center, the apprehension about judgment originates from our natural requirement for acknowledgment and having a place. It is human instinct to look for association and endorsement from everyone around us. Notwithstanding, when this craving for acknowledgment undermines our genuineness, it turns into an enclosure that limits our actual selves. Perceiving this trepidation as a typical human encounter is the most vital phase in beating it. It's essential to figure out that everybody, eventually, wrestles with the apprehension about being judged, however not every person permits it to direct their lives.

The Effect of Living in Dread: Living under the shadow of this dread can have significant results. It smothers our development, restricts our true capacity, and prompts a daily existence loaded up with laments over unfulfilled dreams and unexpressed bits of insight. At the point when we focus on others' perspectives over our genuineness, we double-cross our actual selves, prompting disappointment and misery. The acknowledgment that living in feeling of dread toward judgment is undeniably more choking than the actual judgment is a strong inspiration for change.

Methodologies for Conquering the Trepidation: The excursion to defeating the apprehension about judgment starts with self-empathy and understanding. Perceive that your value isn't dependent upon others' endorsement. Embrace the thought that being consistent with yourself is the groundwork of real joy and satisfaction. Here are functional moves toward assist you with moving past this apprehension:

•Self-reflection: Invest energy figuring out your qualities, convictions, and how validness affects you. This clearness will engage you to stand firm in your personality.

•Little demonstrations of boldness: Begin by offering your actual viewpoints, sentiments, and inclinations in low-stakes circumstances. These little triumphs assemble certainty and strength.

•Look for steady conditions: Encircle yourself with individuals who appreciate and energize validness. Their help can support your mental fortitude to be consistent with yourself.

•Acknowledgment of defect: Perceive that nobody, including yourself, is great. Embracing your defects as a feature of your one of a kind self can free you from the feeling of dread toward judgment.

The Commitment of True Residing: Conquering the anxiety toward judgment makes the way for a daily existence where you are allowed to act naturally, proudly and without requirement. It's a day to day existence where your activities, decisions, and communications are as one with your actual self. This genuineness brings a feeling of harmony, certainty, and satisfaction that far offsets the transitory inconvenience of confronting judgment. It permits you to live completely, embracing potential open doors and encounters with an open heart.

Let the apprehension about judgment be a test to survive, not a hindrance to your realness. By confronting this trepidation with boldness and empathy, you prepare for an existence of credibility, a day to day existence that is genuinely your own. Keep in mind, the main endorsement you really want to live legitimately is your own.

The Snare of Examination: Diagramming Your Remarkable Way

During a time where the features of others' resides are nevertheless a parchment away, the snare of examination has never been more common. An entanglement captures numerous on their excursion toward legitimacy, driving us to quantify our value, accomplishments, and progress against those of others. This persistent correlation can slant our view of ourselves, decreasing our feeling of significant worth and blurring our genuine way. Perceiving and liberating ourselves from the grasp of correlation is essential for anybody looking to carry on with a day to day existence consistent with their own longings, desires, and values.

The Idea of Correlation: Examination, at its center, is a criminal of delight. It cheapens our capacity to see the value in our own excursion, with its special promising and less promising times, by focusing our look on another person's way. The risk lies not in seeing the distinctions between our lives and others' nevertheless in permitting those distinctions to characterize our self-esteem. It's crucial to comprehend that the arranged lives we see via online entertainment or catch wind of in passing are simple pieces of the real world, frequently absent any and all the battles and mishaps that go with any advantageous undertaking.

Grasping Its Effect: The propensity for examination can prompt a bunch of gloomy feelings — jealousy, hatred, and an unavoidable insecurity. It can cause our accomplishments to feel less huge and our disappointments more articulated. This slanted point of view hurts our confidence as well as frustrates our capacity to seek after our bona fide wants. It traps us in a pattern of needing and making progress toward what others have, as opposed to looking for what really satisfies us.

Getting away from the Correlation Trap: Breaking liberated from the pattern of examination requires a purposeful change in concentration and point of view. Here are methodologies to assist you with getting away from this snare and recover your identity:

•Develop appreciation: Routinely recognizing what you're thankful for in your own life can assist with decreasing the desire to think about. Appreciation takes our consideration back to the overflow present in our lives, encouraging happiness and appreciation for our special process.

•Embrace your distinction: Perceive and praise your interesting characteristics, assets, and achievements. Keep in mind, no other person has similar mix of gifts, encounters, and points of view that you do. Your independence is your power.

•Limit openness to triggers: Be aware of what virtual entertainment and certain conditions mean for your inclination to analyze. Restricting openness or arranging your feeds to move instead of impel examination can be useful.

•Center around your own objectives and progress: Divert your energy towards your self-improvement and yearnings. Putting forth and accomplishing your own objectives, in light of the main thing to you, is definitely more compensating than pursuing another person's meaning of achievement.

The Prize of Bona fide Living: Diagramming your way, directed by your qualities, interests, and goals, is the substance of living really. It's an excursion checked not by how well you stack facing others yet by how genuine you stay to yourself. At the point when you free yourself from the snare of examination, you make the way for certifiable satisfaction and satisfaction. You permit yourself to investigate, develop, and prevail in your own particular manner.

Embracing your novel process, with every one of its exciting bends in the road, is a festival of your valid self. It's an affirmation that your life, with its particular difficulties and wins, is sufficient. Relinquish examination, and you'll find that the main individual you should be preferable over is the individual you were yesterday. This is the way to a genuinely valid life.

Relinquishing Hairsplitting: The Opportunity of Defect

Hairsplitting, frequently camouflaged as an upright quest for greatness, can turn into a huge hindrance to living really. A determined journey for perfection sets unreasonable guidelines, prompting self-analysis, feeling of dread toward disappointment, and at last, a removing from our actual selves. Perceiving and delivering the hold of compulsiveness is fundamental for anybody planning to embrace their true character, considering a daily existence improved by development, learning, and certified satisfaction.

The Deception of Flawlessness: Hairsplitting blossoms with the deception that there exists a condition of being where mix-ups are non-existent, and each activity adjusts perfectly with our assumptions. This pursuit, but respectable it might show up, traps us in a pattern of endless disappointment. It causes us to accept that our value is dependent upon our capacity to accomplish flawlessness, disregarding the intrinsic worth of the excursion and the illustrations learned through blemish.

The Outcomes of Pursuing Flawlessness: The results of a fussbudget outlook reach out a long ways past a simple drive for greatness. It can prompt tarrying, where the apprehension about not fulfilling these unreasonable guidelines deadens us from making a move. It breeds a decent outlook, where we view our capacities as static and dread any test that might uncover our blemishes. Above all, it distances us from our legitimate selves, as we become more worried about the presence of flawlessness than with real self-articulation and development.

Embracing Blemish: The excursion to conquering compulsiveness starts with embracing defect, not as an imperfection, but rather as a vital piece of the human experience. Here are moves toward develop this acknowledgment:

•Reexamine your viewpoint: Perceive that slip-ups and disappointments are not indications of shortcoming but rather open doors for development and learning. They are inescapable achievements on the way to progress and self-disclosure.

•Put forth sensible objectives: Go for the gold, flawlessness. Setting reachable, sensible objectives energizes activity and celebrates steady enhancements, cultivating a development mentality.

•Practice self-sympathy: Indulge yourself with a similar benevolence and understanding you would offer a companion. Recognize your endeavors and progress, and advise yourself that flawlessness is an unreachable and superfluous objective.

•Look for criticism for development: View input not as a study of your value but rather as significant contribution for your proceeded with improvement. It's an instrument to assist you with improving, adjust, and develop.

The Opportunity Tracked down in Blemish: Relinquishing compulsiveness divulges the opportunity to live truly, to face challenges, and to communicate our thoughts completely and really. It frees us from the willful shackles that limit our true capacity and diminishes our light. In this opportunity, we track down the space to develop, to analyze, and to commit errors without the smashing gauge

Managing Outer Tensions: Remaining Valid Notwithstanding Assumptions

In our excursion toward credibility, outer tensions — be they cultural standards, social assumptions, or familial requests — pose a potential threat, creating long shaded areas over our way. These tensions can form us into shapes that fit conveniently inside acknowledged limits, yet feel outsider to our actual selves. Figuring out how to explore and oppose these outer powers is significant for anybody trying to carry on with a day to day existence that is really their own, a daily existence that mirrors their actual personality and values.

The Heaviness of Outer Assumptions: Outside tensions can be guileful, meshing their direction into the texture of our lives, frequently without our cognizant mindfulness. They direct what achievement resembles, how we ought to act, and even who we ought to be. This impact can lead us to settle on decisions that adjust more to cultural endorsement than with our own longings and dreams. The outcome is a day to day existence that might seem satisfying from an external perspective however feels empty at its center.

Distinguishing Outer Tensions: The most vital phase in managing outside pressures is to perceive their presence. This requires thoughtfulness and an eagerness to scrutinize the intentions behind our decisions. Is it true that we are chasing after a specific profession, way of life, or relationship since it really impacts us, or on the grounds that it measures up to the assumptions of others? Recognizing these tensions is vital for understanding how they impact our choices and, likewise, our validness.

Systems for Opposing Outside Tensions: Opposing outer tensions requests boldness and a relentless obligation to one's self. Here are systems to assist with strengthening your purpose:

•Explain your qualities and needs: Understanding the main thing to you gives a safeguard against the impact of outside pressures. It assists you explore choices with a reasonable internal compass, grounded in your own qualities and needs.

•Put down stopping points: Laying out limits is a strong method for safeguarding your space and decisions from the infringement of cultural assumptions. It includes figuring out how to say no, to focus on your prosperity, and to respect your legitimate way.

•Look for strong networks: Encircle yourself with people and networks that regard and empower credibility. The help of similar individuals can reinforce your certainty to live as indicated by your actual self, giving an offset to outer tensions.

•Embrace your exceptional excursion: Perceive that your way may not seem as though any other person's — and that is not simply OK, it's delightful. Embracing your one of a kind excursion permits you to commend your independence and fight the temptation to adjust to outer molds.

The Freedom of Validness: Liberating yourself from the hold of outer tensions is a demonstration of freedom. It makes the way for a daily existence where your decisions mirror your actual self, not a reverberation of cultural assumptions. This opportunity isn't without its difficulties, as venturing beyond congruity can prompt analysis or misconception. However, the harmony and satisfaction that come from living really far offset the distress of challenging assumptions.

Living really even with outside pressures is a demonstration of your solidarity and obligation to your actual self. It's an excursion set apart by the boldness to remain solitary, the strength to endure analysis, and the insight to observe your own way. As you explore this excursion, recollect that the main endorsement you genuinely need is your own. In this acknowledgment lies the way in to an existence of legitimacy, a daily existence where outer tensions never again direct your decisions, yet rather, where your decisions enlighten your credible self.

Self-Uncertainty and Weakness: Developing Trust in Your Valid Self

At the junction of our excursion toward validness, we frequently experience the impressive boundaries of self-uncertainty and frailty. These inside enemies murmur inquiries of our value and challenge the legitimacy of our actual selves, creating shaded areas of wavering on our way. Defeating these questions is vital for anybody trying to live genuinely, as it permits us to embrace our character with certainty and push ahead with conviction in the existence we decide to lead.

Grasping the Foundations of Self-Uncertainty: Self-uncertainty and instability frequently originate from an intricate interaction of previous encounters, disappointments, and the assimilation of outer decisions. They blossom with examination and the apprehension about not comparing apparent norms of progress or value. Perceiving these sentiments as normal human encounters, as opposed to novel individual shortfalls, can decrease their power, offering us the most important move toward recovering our confidence.

The Effect of Uncertainty on Realness: When we permit self-uncertainty and frailty to direct our activities, we deceive our valid selves. We could avoid amazing open doors that line up with our interests, quietness our voices when we have something critical to say, or even leave our fantasies inspired by a paranoid fear of disappointment.

This admission as far as possible our true capacity as well as distances us from the embodiment of who we genuinely are.

Procedures for Building Certainty: Building trust in our credible selves is a continuous cycle, requiring persistence, self-empathy, and persevering exertion. Here are commonsense moves toward sustain your self-conviction:

•Commend your accomplishments: Carve out opportunity to recognize and praise your victories, regardless of how little. These triumphs, when perceived, can fabricate a groundwork of certainty that lessens self-question.

•Attest your value: Routinely avow your worth and worth, autonomous of outside accomplishments or approval. Certifications can reshape your inner exchange, cultivating a healthy identity conviction that upholds legitimate living.

•Embrace weakness: Perceive that weakness is a strength, not a shortcoming. Being open about your feelings of dread and frailties can prompt further associations with others and a more grounded identity.

•Challenge negative self-talk: Become aware of the basic internal voice that energizes self-question. Challenge these negative considerations with proof of your abilities and worth, and supplant them with additional strong and empowering stories.

•Look for learning experiences: View difficulties as any open doors for development instead of dangers to your value. Drawing in with new encounters can assemble versatility, decrease dread, and reinforce trust in your capacity to explore the unexplored world.

The Compensation of Conquering Self-Uncertainty: Beating self-uncertainty and frailty is an extraordinary piece of the excursion toward realness. It engages you to stand immovably in your personality, to seek after your interests with boldness, and to carry on with a daily existence that is consistent with yourself. The certainty acquired through defying these inward obstructions enlightens your way, permitting you to push ahead with reason and happiness.

As you keep on exploring the intricacies of living really, recall that self-uncertainty and instability are nevertheless shadows — shadows that lose their power when confronted with the radiance of mindfulness, acknowledgment, and boldness. Developing trust in your bona fide self empowers you to embrace life's bunch potential open doors with receptiveness and excitement, secure in the information that you are sufficient, similarly as you are. This certainty isn't simply the shortfall of uncertainty; it is the presence of confidence in your own value and the worth of your exceptional excursion.

| 3 |

Chapter 3: Cultivating Self-Awareness

Care Works on: Arousing to the Present

In the clamoring beat of present day life, our mindfulness frequently skims the outer layer of our encounters, leaving the profundities of our internal identities neglected. Care rehearses offer an entryway to developing our mindfulness, welcoming us to connect completely with the current second. This commitment enlightens the unpredictable scene of our viewpoints, feelings, and sensations, uncovering the substance of who we are underneath the layers of everyday interruptions.

The Substance of Care: Care is the specialty of focusing, deliberately, right now, and without judgment. It is a training established in old practices, yet its importance is immortal, filling in as an offset to the frequently excited speed of contemporary life. Through care, we develop a nature of consideration that can change our relationship with ourselves and our general surroundings.

Rehearsing Care: The act of care can be incorporated into day to day existence through different strategies, each intriguing us to turn out to be more mindful of the current second:

•Careful Relaxing: This basic practice includes concentrating on the breath. As you breathe in and breathe out, notice the vibes of breathing, involving them as an anchor to the present. At the point when your psyche meanders, delicately guide it back to the breath.

•Body Output Contemplation: This procedure empowers a deliberate excursion through the body, focusing on areas of pressure and unwinding. It encourages a more profound association with the actual self and can uncover how feelings manifest in the body.

•Careful Perception: Pick an article from your current circumstance and concentrate on it. Notice it as though interestingly, taking note of its tones, shapes, surfaces, and characteristics. This training levels up our skill to see subtleties and value the lavishness of our tangible encounters.

•Careful Tuning in: Take part in discussions with full presence, tuning in without arranging your reaction. Tune in with the expectation to comprehend, not to answer. This type of careful listening can develop your associations with others and upgrade your sympathy.

The Advantages of Care: The advantages of coordinating care into day to day existence are complex. It can lessen pressure and uneasiness by breaking the pattern of constant rumination. It upgrades close to home guideline, assisting us answer circumstances with clearness instead of respond indiscreetly. Besides, care practices can further develop focus and mental adaptability, empowering us to connect all the more completely with assignments and imaginative undertakings.

Developing Mindfulness: At its center, care is an excursion internal. It offers a way to finding the subtleties of our inward world, from the back and forth movement of our feelings to the examples of our viewpoints. By noticing ourselves with consideration and interest, we figure out how to grasp our responses, inclinations, and abhorrences. This understanding is the foundation of mindfulness, enlightening our valid selves and directing us toward living all the more intentionally and legitimately.

Embracing care is an encouragement to dial back and relish life, to meet ourselves with sympathy and interest. A training doesn't look to change what our identity is yet rather to uncover our actual selves, each second in turn. As we develop care, we stir to the lavishness of our inward scene, leaving on an excursion of self-revelation that is both significant and groundbreaking.

Journaling for Self-Revelation: The Composed Way to Understanding

In the journey for mindfulness, journaling arises as an integral asset, offering a confidential space for reflection, investigation, and revelation. It is the demonstration of interpreting considerations, sentiments, and encounters into words, giving an unmistakable structure to the immaterial. This act of self-articulation helps with handling life altering's situations as well as fills in as a mirror mirroring the profundities of our inward world. Through journaling, we set out on a composed excursion toward understanding ourselves all the more profoundly, uncovering bits of knowledge that guide us on the way to genuineness.

The Act of Journaling: Journaling for self-disclosure is an adaptable and individual practice, versatile to the requirements and rhythms of the person. It can take many structures, from everyday reflections and appreciation records to investigations of dreams and difficulties. The key is consistency and trustworthiness, permitting the diary to turn into a confided in buddy in your excursion of mindfulness.

•Intelligent Journaling: This includes expounding on your day, your connections, and your sentiments. It's a method for handling occasions and perceive designs in your viewpoints and ways of behaving.

•Appreciation Journaling: Routinely taking note of what you're grateful for can move your concentration based on what's missing to what's bountiful in your life, encouraging energy and happiness.

•Continuous flow Composing: Composing without control or judgment can uncover contemplations and sentiments you weren't intentionally mindful of, offering significant bits of knowledge into your internal identity.

•Objective and Dream Journaling: Articulating your yearnings explains what you genuinely want and uncovers the qualities and inspirations that drive you.

Advantages of Journaling: The demonstration of journaling offers various advantages for upgrading mindfulness and encouraging self-improvement:

•Reliable: Composing unwinds complex contemplations, making it more obvious and address them.

•Profound Delivery: Communicating feelings through composing can be soothing, assisting with overseeing and ease pressure, uneasiness, and bitterness.

•Self-Reflection: Routinely inspecting your encounters and feelings through journaling supports further self-reflection, prompting more prominent mindfulness and understanding.

•Critical thinking: Journaling can be a device for figuring out through issues, permitting you to move toward difficulties from various points and reveal clever fixes.

Developing a Journaling Propensity: To coordinate journaling into your life, begin by saving a couple of moments every day for composing. Pick a medium that feels great, whether a customary scratch pad or a computerized application, and make an inviting space that moves reflection. Move toward your diary with an open heart and psyche, liberated from the strain of flawlessness. Keep in mind, the objective isn't persuasiveness yet validness.

The Excursion Inside: Journaling for self-disclosure is in excess of a training; it's an excursion. With each word composed, you strip back layers, uncovering insights about your longings, fears, delights, and distresses. This course of self-investigation can be groundbreaking, prompting a more profound comprehension of what your identity is and the way that you need to explore the world.

As you proceed to diary, you fabricate a guide of your inward scene, set apart by the achievements of your development and the pathways to your fantasies. This guide guides you toward living all the more genuinely, lined up with your actual self. In the pages of your diary, you track down words, however an impression of your excursion toward mindfulness and the pith of what your identity is.

Criticism and Reflection: The Reflection of Development

In the mosaic of mindfulness, criticism from others fills in as a mirror, reflecting parts of ourselves we might ignore or battle to see. It gives an outer point of view that can challenge our self-discernment, empowering development and more profound comprehension. Combined with individual reflection, criticism turns into a strong impetus for realness, permitting us to see the diverse idea of our being and to adjust all the more intimately with our actual selves.

The Worth of Input: Criticism, when offered helpfully and got transparently, can enlighten stowed away qualities and uncover regions for development. It goes about as a scaffold between how we see ourselves and how others experience us, offering bits of knowledge that can develop our mindfulness. Whether it comes from partners, companions, or family, input is a gift that, when embraced, impels us toward self-improvement.

Exploring Criticism: To tackle the force of input in your excursion of self-disclosure, think about the accompanying methodologies:

•Search out input: Proactively request criticism from those you trust frankly and steady. Outline your solicitation around unambiguous regions you're chipping away at, and be available to what you hear.

•Tune in without safeguard: Getting criticism can summon protectiveness, particularly assuming it addresses touchy regions. Endeavor to tune in with a receptive outlook, isolating your healthy identity worth from the data being shared.

•Consider the input: Subsequent to getting criticism, find opportunity to reflect. Consider what impacts you and what doesn't, and why. Considering input permits you to filter through what is important and what might be impacted by the provider's own discernments or predispositions.

•Coordinate criticism with self-reflection: Join bits of knowledge from input with your own self-reflection. This coordination can offer a more adjusted perspective on yourself, featuring areas of compatibility and inconsistency between your self-discernment and how others see you.

The Job of Reflection: Reflection is the inward partner to outside input. It includes going internal to analyze our considerations, feelings, and responses, taking into account both where we succeed and where we could get to the next level. Reflection develops how we might interpret ourselves, cultivating development and self-empathy. It urges us to pose examining inquiries: For what reason did I respond that way? What does this feeling inform me regarding my requirements or values? How might I adjust my activities all the more intimately with my credible self?

Developing Through Criticism and Reflection: The interaction among input and reflection is a powerful course of compromise, talking and tuning in, searching externally and turning internal. It's a dance that, when taken part in mindfully, can prompt significant self-improvement and upgraded mindfulness. Through this cycle, we learn not exclusively to acknowledge ourselves, with every one of our intricacies and logical inconsistencies, yet additionally to embrace the excursion of turning out to be all the more legitimately us.

Criticism and reflection offer a pathway to realness, giving clearness and understanding that guide our decisions and activities. As we figure out how to get criticism with effortlessness and reflect with trustworthiness, we open ourselves to the vast potential outcomes of development. This excursion of self-revelation is generally difficult, yet it is profoundly fulfilling, driving us to a more full, more legitimate life. In the reflection of criticism and reflection, we find the individual we are, however the individual we seek to be.

The capacity to appreciate individuals on a profound level: Exploring the Scene of Sentiments

In the mission for mindfulness, understanding and dealing with our feelings is likened to dominating the language of our own hearts. This dominance, known as the ability to understand anyone on a deeper level, outfits us with the devices to explore the mind boggling scene of our sentiments, improving our connections with ourselves as well as other people. The capacity to understand people on a deeper level is the extension between simple mindfulness and the capacity to act carefully upon that mindfulness, making it a foundation of living truly.

The Parts of The capacity to understand individuals on a profound level: The capacity to understand people on a profound level involves a few key parts, each adding to a more profound comprehension and more viable administration of our close to home world:

•Mindfulness: The capacity to perceive and figure out your own feelings, the most vital phase in ability to understand people on a profound level, establishes the groundwork for any remaining perspectives. It includes distinguishing how feelings impact your considerations and activities and perceiving the effect of your close to home state on your way of behaving.

•Self-guideline: Expanding upon mindfulness, self-guideline includes dealing with your feelings in solid ways, communicating them properly, and not permitting them to overpower your considerations or activities. It's tied in with practicing control and diverting problematic feelings and motivations.

•Compassion: The ability to comprehend and discuss the thoughts of another is vital for building solid, valid connections. Compassion reaches out past simple compassion, including a profound, veritable association with others' personal encounters.

•Interactive abilities: Successful correspondence, compromise, and the capacity to fabricate and keep up with connections are all essential for the interactive abilities part of the capacity to understand anyone on a profound level. These abilities permit us to explore social circumstances with effortlessness and genuineness.

Creating The capacity to understand individuals on a profound level: The excursion to improving ability to appreciate people at their core is progressing, a way of consistent learning and development. Here are techniques to develop these fundamental abilities:

•Careful perception of feelings: Work on noticing your feelings without judgment, basically taking note of their presence and taking into account their sources. This care can increase your profound mindfulness.

•Practice close to home guideline procedures: Strategies like profound breathing, reflection, or stopping prior to answering can assist with areas of strength for overseeing, giving space to pick the proper behavior.

•Develop sympathy: Attempt to see circumstances according to others' viewpoints, effectively listen when individuals talk about their thoughts, and answer with empathy and understanding.

•Work on friendly cooperations: Work on your relational abilities, figure out how to listen effectively, and work on being available in discussions. Look for input on your social associations and be available to development and change.

The Job of The capacity to understand people on a deeper level in Bona fide Living: The ability to understand individuals on a profound level is in excess of a bunch of abilities — it's an approach to drawing in with the world that praises the full range of human inclination. By getting it and dealing with our feelings, we can pursue choices that are in arrangement with our actual selves, explore the intricacies of associations with respectability, and answer life's difficulties with versatility and elegance.

In the domain of mindfulness, the capacity to understand people on a deeper level goes about as a directing light, enlightening the way to credibility. It permits us to live with a feeling of direction and satisfaction, embracing our feelings as wellsprings of solidarity and intelligence. As we fill in ability to appreciate people at their core, we track down that our ability for delight, compassion, and association grows, enhancing our experience of life and developing comprehension we might interpret ourselves as well as other people.

Embracing the capacity to understand individuals on a deeper level is an excursion toward the core of realness, an excursion that welcomes us to investigate the profundity of our feelings and the broadness of our human experience. It is an excursion certainly worth taking, for in the scene of sentiments, we find the embodiment of what our identity is and the magnificence of what we can turn into.

Making an Individual Vision: Outlining the Course to Your Legitimate Self

At the core of mindfulness lies the capacity to imagine a day to day existence that is profoundly lined up with your most genuine self — a daily existence that resounds with your guiding principle, interests, and reason. Making an individual vision is a demonstration of clearness and mental fortitude, a statement of where you wish your life to take. It fills in as a directing star, enlightening the way toward legitimacy, and enabling you to go with decisions that reflect who you are at your center.

The Quintessence of an Individual Vision: An individual vision is something other than a bunch of objectives or goals; it is a far reaching image of the everyday routine you try to experience, enveloping all parts of your being. It explains your most elevated esteems, your most significant longings, and the effect you wish to have on your general surroundings. Making this vision requires thoughtfulness and creative mind, an eagerness to dream strongly and to stand up to the bits of insight of your current reality.

Moves toward Making Your Own Vision: Making an individual vision includes a few key stages, each intended to extend how you might interpret yourself and to explain your goals:

1. Reflect on Your Qualities: Start by recognizing the qualities that are mean quite a bit to you. What standards guide your choices? What do you rely on? Your qualities act as the underpinning of your own vision, guaranteeing that it mirrors your actual self.

2. Explore Your Interests: Think about what exercises, subjects, or causes light your excitement and give you pleasure. Your interests are marks of where your heart lies and integrating them into your vision adds liveliness and reason to your life.

3. Envision Your Optimal Future: Permit yourself to dream about the future without requirements. What does your ideal life resemble concerning connections, vocation, self-improvement, and commitments to society? Be all around as definite as could

be expected, envisioning the way that it feels to carry on with this life.

4. Identify Objectives and Activities: Separate your vision into feasible objectives and explicit activities that will push you toward this optimal future. What steps could you at any point take today, this week, or this year to carry you nearer to your vision?

5. Write It Down: Commit your own vision to paper, making an unmistakable report that you can allude to and update on a case by case basis. Composing sets your responsibility and fills in as a consistent sign of where you wish to take.

Living Your Own Vision: Your own vision is a living record, one that develops as you develop and acquire further experiences into your credible self. It requires creation as well as responsibility — obligation to living in arrangement with your vision, to pursuing decisions that mirror your qualities and interests, and to exploring life's vulnerabilities with your vision as your compass.

Embracing your own vision enables you to live with goal and reason. It changes the manner in which you decide, how you designate your significant investment, and how you draw in with your general surroundings. Your vision turns into the focal point through which you view your life, sifting through interruptions and zeroing in on the main thing.

The Excursion Ahead: Making and living your own vision is an excursion of change. It welcomes you to investigate the profundities of your longings, to face the real factors of your ongoing circumstance, and to move toward the everyday routine you wish to experience. This excursion is generally difficult, yet it is profoundly fulfilling, for it prompts a daily existence that is legitimately yours — a daily existence that reverberates with your most genuine self, loaded up with reason, energy, and satisfaction.

As you outline the course to your valid self, let your own vision guide you, focusing light on the way forward and helping you to remember the daily routine you seek to experience. Chasing this vision, you find your objective as well as the lavishness of the actual excursion, an excursion set apart by development, self-disclosure, and the delight of being genuinely you.

| 4 |

Chapter 4: Setting Authentic Goals

Adjusting Objectives to Values: The Core of Real Yearnings

Chasing after a valid life, defining objectives that reverberate profoundly with our own qualities is foremost. This arrangement guarantees that our goals are achievements we mean to accomplish as well as are articulations of our most genuine selves, reflecting what we hold generally dear. The most common way of adjusting our objectives to our qualities is both an excursion of contemplation and a guarantee to carrying on with an existence of direction and significance.

Understanding Your Basic beliefs: The most vital phase in adjusting your objectives to your qualities is to characterize what those values are obviously. These are the rules that guide your choices, shape your convictions, and characterize a big motivator for you. They could incorporate honesty, empathy, development, family, or imagination, among others. Recognizing your guiding principle requires fair reflection on the main thing to you, past cultural assumptions or outside pressures.

The Meaning of Arrangement: When your objectives are together as one with your qualities, seeking after them brings a feeling of satisfaction and fulfillment that rises above the actual accomplishment. This arrangement guarantees that your way is driven by inspirations that are truly critical to you, instead of by momentary longings or the impact of others. It pervades your excursion with importance and mixes your accomplishments with a feeling of genuine achievement.

Laying out Bona fide Objectives: Valid objectives are those that mirror your qualities and add to the vision you have for your life. They are private, significant, and established in what makes you extraordinarily you. To define bona fide objectives, think about the accompanying advances:

1. Reflect on Your Qualities: Return to your guiding principle and consider how they manifest in your life. What does achievement resemble inside the system of these qualities?
2. Visualize Your Future: Envision your optimal future exhaustively. How can it epitomize your qualities? What are you doing, and how can it cause you to feel?
3. Identify Explicit Objectives: In view of your appearance and representation, distinguish explicit objectives that line up with your qualities. These objectives ought to be concrete, quantifiable, and tied straightforwardly to the qualities you've distinguished.
4. Evaluate and Change: Consistently assess your objectives to guarantee they stay lined up with your advancing qualities. Be ready to change them as you develop and as how you might interpret yourself extends.

The Force of Compatible Living: Living in harmoniousness with your qualities and objectives is enabling. It gives a reasonable bearing and a feeling of motivation, settling on choice making simpler and more significant. At the point when your activities are lined up with your most profound convictions, you experience an amicable presence where each work feels huge, and each accomplishment is a festival of your bona fide self.

Embracing the Excursion: Adjusting your objectives to your qualities is definitely not a one-time occasion however a nonstop course of arrangement and realignment. It requires care, devotion, and the fortitude to settle on decisions that are consistent with yourself. This excursion, while testing, is amazingly fulfilling. It prompts a day to day existence lived with aim, a day to day existence that is genuinely yours, loaded up with enthusiasm, reason, and significant fulfillment.

As you leave on defining your valid objectives, recollect that the genuine proportion of progress lies not in that frame of mind of the actual objectives but rather chasing a day to day existence that really reflects what your identity is. In this arrangement among objectives and values, you track down the substance of genuineness, the delight of living consistent with yourself, and the harmony that comes from realizing your life is an immediate articulation of what you esteem most.

Separating Obstructions: Procedures for Beating Deterrents to True Objectives

The excursion toward accomplishing our genuine objectives is seldom without challenge. En route, we experience obstructions — both inward and outside — that can upset our advancement. These obstructions, nonetheless, are not unfavorable. With the right methodologies, we can explore through them, guaranteeing that our way stays lined up with our most profound qualities and goals. This section investigates functional ways to deal with defeating the boundaries that stand among us and the satisfaction of our valid objectives.

Distinguishing Normal Boundaries: The most vital phase in conquering impediments is to remember them. Obstructions can take many structures, from self-uncertainty and apprehension about inability to outside pressures and strategic limitations. Understanding the idea of these hindrances and their starting point is critical for conceiving successful systems to defeat them.

Developing Strength: Versatility is the foundation of exploring difficulties. It's the capacity to return from mishaps, to adjust and persist despite challenges. Developing versatility includes fostering a development outlook, one that perspectives challenges as any open doors for learning and development as opposed to unrealistic snags.

•Embrace Disappointment as an Instructor: Disappointment isn't something contrary to progress yet a piece of the excursion toward it. Every mishap offers important illustrations that can direct future endeavors. Embracing disappointment with receptiveness and interest cultivates versatility and prepares for advancement and improvement.

•Foster an Encouraging group of people: Encircle yourself with people who support your real objectives and values. A solid encouraging group of people can give support, exhortation, and useful assistance when impediments emerge. Knowing you're in good company in your process can reinforce your strength and assurance.

•Practice Taking care of oneself: Exploring difficulties can be burdening, both intellectually and actually. Focusing on taking care of oneself guarantees that you have the energy and mental clearness expected to actually address snags. Standard activity, sufficient rest, and careful practices like reflection can upgrade your strength by keeping you grounded and centered.

Key Critical thinking: Beating deterrents frequently requires innovative critical thinking. This includes separating boundaries into reasonable parts, investigating different arrangements, and going ahead with potentially dangerous courses of action.

•Recognize Explicit Difficulties: Dissect the obstruction to figure out its parts. What explicit variables are adding to the test? Separating it can cause it to appear to be not so much overwhelming but rather more sensible.

•Create Numerous Arrangements: Conceptualize different techniques to defeat every part of the test. Breaking new ground can uncover imaginative arrangements that might not have been at first clear.

•Carry out and Assess: Pick the most encouraging arrangements and execute them. A short time later, assess their viability. What functioned admirably? Really what didn't? This course of experimentation is fundamental for tracking down the best way ahead.

Keeping up with Energy: Diligence is critical to defeating hindrances. Keeping up with energy, in any event, when progress appears to be slow, is fundamental for accomplishing your objectives. Celebrate little triumphs en route, and help yourself to remember the more deeply esteems driving your endeavors. These updates can reignite your inspiration and responsibility, pushing you through times of stagnation or uncertainty.

Embracing the Excursion: The excursion toward credible objectives is basically as significant as the actual objectives. Every hindrance defeat is a step in the right direction in your self-improvement, a demonstration of your versatility, and a more profound arrangement with your qualities. By embracing the difficulties and review them as necessary pieces of the excursion, you change obstructions into open doors for development.

In defeating these hindrances, we draw nearer to our valid objectives as well as extend how we might interpret ourselves and our capacities. The methodologies framed in this part are not only devices for accomplishing objectives yet are rehearses for carrying on with a daily existence that is genuinely credible, strong, and satisfying.

The Force of Little Advances: Embracing Gradual Advancement Toward Large Changes

Leaving on the excursion toward our genuine objectives, particularly those that pose a potential threat and aggressive, can frequently feel overwhelming. The size of what we try to accomplish may eclipse our faith in our capacity to succeed. However, the key to understanding these fabulous dreams lies not in a solitary, great jump, but rather in the force of little, purposeful advances. This methodology of embracing steady advancement changes the excursion into a progression of reasonable, reachable errands, every one structure on the last toward the final location of our genuine yearnings.

Grasping Steady Advancement: Gradual advancement is the act of separating general objectives into more modest, noteworthy stages. This technique recognizes that change is a cycle, not an occasion, and that each critical accomplishment is the total consequence of numerous little endeavors. By zeroing in on what can be achieved temporarily, we keep up with energy and cultivate a pride that powers our inspiration for the excursion ahead.

Setting Attainable Achievements: The most vital phase in utilizing the force of little advances is to frame reachable achievements that lead to your bigger objective. These achievements ought to be explicit, quantifiable, and time-bound, giving clear focuses to plan to. For instance, in the event that you want to compose a book, an achievement could be to compose a section every month or to devote a particular number of hours to composing every week. These more modest targets cause the bigger objective to feel more feasible and give a guide to your endeavors.

Observing Little Triumphs: Every achievement came to is a triumph by its own doing and merits acknowledgment. Commending these achievements supports positive way of behaving and keeps inspiration high. Whether it's indulging yourself with something uniquely great or just pausing for a minute to ponder your advancement, recognizing your triumphs, regardless of how little, is essential for supporting energy.

Gaining from Each Step: As you explore the way of gradual advancement, each step offers important illustrations. Considering what functioned admirably and what didn't permits you to change your system depending on the situation. This consistent circle of activity, reflection, and change is a strong system for development and learning. It guarantees that you are drawing nearer to your objective as well as refining your methodology in view of genuine experience.

The Compound Impact of Little Activities: The genuine wizardry of little advances lies in their compound impact over the long haul. Like individual brushstrokes adding to a show-stopper, each activity you take expands upon the last, continuously rejuvenating your vision. This aggregate effect highlights the significance of consistency and diligence, advising us that advancement, regardless of how steady, is still advancement.

Embracing the Excursion: Taking on a mentality that values gradual advancement welcomes us to embrace the excursion toward our objectives with persistence and perseverance. It moves our concentration from the overwhelming ultimate objective to the sensible advances that lead there, making the cycle more pleasant and less overpowering. By commending each step, gaining from the excursion, and confiding in the compound impact of our activities, we enable ourselves to accomplish our most legitimate objectives, each little move toward turn.

In this hug of gradual advancement, we track down a technique for accomplishing objectives as well as a way of thinking for living really. It instructs us that the way to our fantasies is cleared with persistence, that each work counts, and that, in the amassing of little advances, we track down the solidarity to understand our most prominent yearnings.

Remaining Valid Under Tension: Keeping up with Genuineness Notwithstanding Difficulties

As we venture toward the acknowledgment of our real objectives, we constantly experience snapshots of strain — times when outside requests, assumptions, and, surprisingly, our own questions take steps to mislead us. These minutes test our obligation to our qualities and the credibility of our way. Remaining consistent with ourselves under tension isn't simply a test; it's a significant part of accomplishing our objectives such that respects our actual selves.

Perceiving the Wellsprings of Strain: Tension can radiate from different sources — social assumptions, proficient conditions, individual connections, or assimilated fears of deficiency. Recognizing these tensions and understanding their starting points are the most important moves toward relieving their effect. It includes a cognizant work to perceive which requests line up with our qualities and objectives and which don't.

Reaffirming Your Qualities: despite pressure, the solidarity to stay consistent with ourselves comes from a profound, steady association with our qualities. Returning to and reaffirming these center standards can act as a reference point, directing our choices and activities in any event, when outside powers push us toward similarity. It's tied in with inquiring, "Does this line up with who I am and what I have faith in?" This question turns into an incredible asset for exploring difficulties with trustworthiness.

The Job of Fearlessness: A basic partner in remaining valid under tension is self-assurance — the faith in our capacity to settle on choices that are ideal as far as we're concerned, in any event, when they contradict some common norms. Building fearlessness includes thinking about past triumphs, recognizing our assets, and understanding that our worth doesn't depend on outer approval. The establishment permits us to stand firm in our convictions and act in arrangement with our bona fide selves.

Procedures for Strength: Versatility is the ability to return from difficulty, to adjust and move ahead chasing after our objectives. Developing versatility requires:

•Care: Staying present and mindful assists us with answering strain with clearness instead of respond imprudently.

•Encouraging groups of people: Resting on companions, family, or coaches who get it and backing our bona fide way can give strength and support during testing times.

•Taking care of oneself: Focusing on physical and mental prosperity guarantees we have the energy and strength to confront pressures without undermining our qualities.

Embracing Weakness: Weakness, the readiness to be viewed as we really are, is a strength in keeping up with genuineness under tension. It includes straightforwardly recognizing our battles, questions, and fears, instead of hiding them behind an exterior of insusceptibility. This receptiveness can encourage veritable associations and backing, building up our obligation to our legitimate objectives.

Exploring the Way ahead: Remaining consistent with ourselves under tension is a continuous interaction, one that requires steady watchfulness, reflection, and change. About settling on decisions reverberate with our internal truth, in any event, when the easiest course of action entices us to wander.

Chasing credible objectives, the tensions we face can either redirect us from our way or fortify our purpose. By reaffirming our qualities, building self-assurance, developing versatility, and embracing weakness, we prepare ourselves to explore these difficulties without failing to focus on what our identity is. This relentlessness not just carries us closer to accomplishing our objectives yet additionally guarantees that the excursion mirrors our actual selves, instilled with honesty and realness.

Observing Achievements: Perceiving and Embracing Progress on Your Credible Way

In the excursion toward understanding our valid objectives, the demonstration of praising achievements isn't only a delay for self-compliment; a fundamental practice supports our responsibility, encourages us, and reestablishes our inspiration. Every achievement accomplished is a demonstration of our tirelessness, an impression of our development, and an indication of the headway we've made toward carrying on with a day to day existence that really reverberates with our guiding principle. This festival of progress, both of all shapes and sizes, is a pivotal part of keeping up with force and remaining lined up with our credible selves.

The Significance of Affirmation: Recognizing our accomplishments fills different needs. It approves the work and commitment we've contributed, giving a substantial feeling of achievement. This acknowledgment is particularly significant in long haul pursuits, where a definitive objective might require a very long time to accomplish. By commending the achievements en route, we help ourselves to remember the headway we've made, building up the worth of our excursion and the feasibility of our goals.

Setting Significant Achievements: To successfully celebrate progress, we should initially characterize what is an achievement with regards to our genuine objectives. These markers ought to be significant and intelligent of our qualities, implying the headway toward an objective as well as self-improvement and improvement. Whether it's securing another expertise, beating a test, or settling on a critical choice lined up with our legitimate way, every achievement is a bit nearer to the acknowledgment of our fantasies.

Celebrating in Arrangement with Your Qualities: how we praise our achievements ought to be consistent with our qualities and the quintessence of our bona fide objectives. For some's purposes, festivity could mean offering accomplishments to friends and family, for other people, it could include calm reflection on the excursion up to this point. The key is to pick types of festivity that build up our association with our qualities, improving our feeling of satisfaction and euphoria.

Pondering the Excursion: Commending achievements additionally offers a chance for reflection. It's an opportunity to think back on the way we've voyaged, to see the value in the difficulties we've survived, and to gather bits of knowledge that can illuminate our future heading. This intelligent practice develops our mindfulness, permitting us to change our course on a case by case basis and to reaffirm our obligation to our legitimate yearnings.

The Expanding influence of Festivity: The demonstration of praising our advancement has an expanding influence, moving people around us to seek after their real ways. It shows the force of steadiness, the worth of devotion, and the delight of living in arrangement with one's qualities. Moreover, it cultivates a culture of appreciation and backing inside our networks, empowering aggregate development and accomplishment.

Embracing Each Forward-moving step: In the fabulous embroidery of our lives, every achievement accomplished is a string of variety, adding profundity and extravagance to the general picture. Commending these achievements urges us to embrace each step of our excursion, perceiving that the way to our genuine objectives is cleared with snapshots of win, learning, and development. It helps us that the pursuit to remember validness isn't just about the objective yet about esteeming each insight en route.

As we keep on exploring the way toward our credible objectives, let us make sure to commend the achievements that mark our advancement. In doing as such, we honor our excursion, build up our obligation to our qualities, and draw motivation for the street ahead. Praising achievements isn't simply a transient respite yet an essential practice in living legitimately, one that keeps us associated with our motivation, our development, and the significant delight of chasing after a day to day existence that is genuinely our own.

| 5 |

Chapter 5: Building Authentic Relationships

Weakness as Strength: The Groundwork of True Associations

In the domain of building legitimate connections, weakness arises not as a shortcoming but rather as a significant strength. It is the fearless demonstration of opening our hearts, sharing our actual selves, and embracing the full range of our human experience. This transparency makes ready for more profound associations, cultivating a feeling of trust and grasping that frames the bedrock of any significant relationship.

The Quintessence of Weakness: Weakness includes letting down our watchmen and appearing as we really are, without covers or affectations. It implies sharing our contemplations, sentiments, and encounters — including our feelings of trepidation, dreams, and frailties — with others. This demonstration of transparency can feel overwhelming, as it opens us to the chance of judgment or dismissal. However, it is definitively this hazard that instills weakness with its power, changing it into a conductor for valid association.

Developing Weakness: To develop weakness in connections, we should initially embrace it inside ourselves. This requires self-acknowledgment and the acknowledgment that our defects and battles are fundamental pieces of our humankind. By recognizing and possessing our weaknesses, we set up for certified connections that welcome others to impart their valid selves to us.

•Begin with Self-Reflection: Grasp your own weaknesses by thinking about your feelings of trepidation, trusts, and the parts of yourself you normally keep stowed away. Mindfulness is the most important move toward easily offering your actual self to other people.

•Pick Places of refuge: Offer your weaknesses in conditions and with people where you have a solid sense of reassurance and upheld. Few out of every odd setting or individual will be helpful for true sharing, so it's critical to carefully pick.

•Practice Undivided attention: Be available and really listen when others share their weaknesses with you. Making a space of common regard and understanding supports further associations.

The Harmony Among Weakness and Limits: While weakness is a foundation of true connections, it should be offset with solid limits. Limits assist with safeguarding our prosperity, guaranteeing that our receptiveness doesn't allow us to remain uncovered to damage or abuse. Imparting your limits plainly and regarding those of others is critical in keeping up with connections that are both credible and solid.

The Extraordinary Force of Weakness: Embracing weakness has the ability to change connections. It separates hindrances, cultivates sympathy, and constructs a groundwork of trust that is fundamental for valid associations. Weak communications advise us that we are in good company in our encounters, cultivating a feeling of imparted humankind and extending our securities to other people.

In the excursion toward building legitimate connections, weakness remains as a demonstration of our solidarity and flexibility. It is a challenge to interface on a more profound level, to see and be seen, to cherish and be cherished for who we genuinely are. By embracing weakness, we open ourselves to the lavishness of real associations, finding en route that our most prominent strength lies in our ability to be legitimately ourselves, together.

Legitimate Correspondence: Talking and Tuning in from the Heart

At the center of building and supporting legitimate connections lies the specialty of true correspondence. This type of trade goes past the simple transmission of data; it is an open, fair, and genuine sharing of contemplations and sentiments that cultivates understanding and association. Credible correspondence is portrayed by straightforwardness, genuineness, and a profound regard for one and the other. It is through this certifiable exchange that connections extend, trust is fabricated, and a genuine accord and hearts is accomplished.

The Force of Genuineness: Bona fide correspondence flourishes with trustworthiness. It includes offering your actual viewpoints, sentiments, and goals plainly and straightforwardly, without control or camouflage. This genuineness, be that as it may, isn't obtuse or pernicious; it is tempered with graciousness and thought for different's sentiments. It's tied in with tracking down the boldness to get out whatever should be said while likewise thinking often profoundly about how it lands with the other individual.

The Craft of Undivided attention: Similarly critical to talking your reality is the act of undivided attention. This implies completely focusing on the thing is being expressed as opposed to just trusting that your turn will talk. It includes tuning in with all faculties — focusing to the words as well as to the tone, speed, and feelings behind them. Undivided attention additionally requires compassion, the capacity to imagine the other individual's perspective and figure out their viewpoint, regardless of whether it varies from your own.

Exploring Troublesome Discussions: Legitimate correspondence is generally critical, and frequently generally testing, during troublesome discussions — those that include struggle, conflict, or close to home weakness. Exploring these discussions with genuineness requires a few key procedures:

•Approach with Compassion: Begin from a position of attempting to grasp the other individual's perspective, regardless of whether you conflict.

•Use "I" Proclamations: Express the way that you feel and what you want without finding fault. For instance, "I feel upset when..." rather than "You make me upset because..."

•Look for Shared belief: Search for areas of understanding or shared values that can act as an establishment for settling contrasts.

The Job of Nonverbal Correspondence: Nonverbal signals assume a critical part in legitimate correspondence. Non-verbal communication, eye to eye connection, looks, and manner of speaking can all convey volumes about our actual sentiments and aims. Being aware of these nonverbal signs — both in ourselves and in others — improves our capacity to convey legitimately and to peruse the basic feelings and messages in a discussion.

Encouraging Association Through Validness: The substance of real correspondence lies in its capacity to overcome any barrier between people, making a space where certifiable association and understanding can prosper. By talking and tuning in from the heart, we honor our own reality and the reality of others, laying the preparation for connections that are established in common regard, compassion, and credibility.

In developing the act of genuine correspondence, we advance our connections as well as fill in our own mindfulness and limit with respect to compassion. An excursion requires fortitude, weakness, and a guarantee to truth, yet the prizes — a day to day existence loaded up with significant, profound associations — are inconceivably worth the effort. From the perspective of valid correspondence, we see into the hearts of others as well as into the profundities of our own.

Defining Limits: The Craft of Respecting Yourself As well as other people

In the embroidery of genuine connections, the winding of sound limits is a fundamental string. Limits outline where we end and others start, permitting us to explore our connections with clearness and regard. They are the declaration of our requirements, cutoff points, and values, imparted transparently and maintained with consistency. Defining and regarding limits isn't a boundary to closeness yet an establishment for it, encouraging connections that are deferential together, mindful, and valid.

Grasping Limits: Limits can be personal, physical, scholarly, or time-related, among others. They assist with safeguarding our prosperity, make a place of refuge for our true selves to thrive, and empower us to draw in with others in a sound and conscious way. Understanding your limits includes a profound jump into what feels ideal for you — what you really want to feel regarded, esteemed, and agreeable in your connections.

Conveying Limits: The foundation of defining limits is compelling correspondence. It requires the boldness to communicate your necessities and cutoff points obviously and straightforwardly, without statement of regret. This correspondence ought to be established in genuineness and confidence, conveying your limits in a way that is confident yet humane. For example, saying, "I esteem our time together, however I want to possess some peaceful energy for myself in the nights," sets an unmistakable limit while likewise confirming the significance of the relationship.

Regarding Others' Limits: Similarly however significant as defining your own limits seems to be regarding those set by others. This regard is a demonstration of your obligation to genuine connections, recognizing that every individual's necessities and cutoff points are substantial and significant. By regarding others' limits, you develop a space of shared regard and understanding, where valid associations can flourish.

Exploring Pushback: In defining limits, it's normal to experience opposition or pushback. Some might see limits as a dismissal or a test. Exploring this pushback requires solidness and consolation — repeating the significance of your limits for your prosperity and the strength of the relationship. It's tied in with holding fast, tenderly however fearlessly, building up that limits are not debatable yet fundamental for your validness and bliss.

The Powerful Idea of Limits: Limits are not static; they develop as we develop and our connections change. Ordinary reflection on and change of your limits is vital to guaranteeing they keep on serving your necessities and mirror your genuine self. This continuous interaction is a discourse — inside yourself and with others — about what works and what doesn't, encouraging connections that are dynamic, deferential, and profoundly associated.

The Endowment of Limits: Defining and regarding limits is a significant demonstration of self esteem and regard for other people. It is the acknowledgment that for connections to be truly sustaining, they should respect the distinction and requirements of all included. Limits permit us to cooperate with trustworthiness and respectability, developing our associations and enhancing our lives.

In the excursion toward building valid connections, the specialty of defining limits is crucial. It enables us to reside in arrangement with our qualities and requirements, making spaces where our actual selves are seen, regarded, and appreciated. From the perspective of solid limits, we experience the full profundity and extravagance of our connections, moored in common regard and certifiable association.

Keeping up with Connections: The Consistent Exertion of Supporting Bona fide Associations

The making of legitimate connections is only the start; the pith of their magnificence and profundity lies in their support. Like a nursery, connections require continuous consideration, consideration, and sustenance to flourish. This section investigates the persistent exertion engaged with sustaining true associations, guaranteeing they develop, advance, and stay energetic after some time. It is a pledge to the excursion of developing bonds, confronting difficulties together, and commending the development that comes from shared encounters.

The Significance of Exertion and Responsibility: Supporting valid connections requests exertion and responsibility from all gatherings included. It's tied in with deciding to contribute time, energy, and profound assets into the relationship, in any event, when life gets going or challenges emerge. This responsibility is the dirt wherein the foundations of the relationship can extend, giving solidness and sustenance.

Adjusting to Change: Change is an unavoidable piece of life and connections. As people develop and advance, so too should their connections. Embracing change inside a relationship implies being available to new elements, interests, and approaches to connecting with each other. It requires adaptability, understanding, and a readiness to explore the obscure together. By moving toward change as a chance for development, connections can adjust and thrive in new and startling ways.

Correspondence: The Help of Relationship Support: Progressing, open, and genuine correspondence is fundamental for keeping up with credible connections. It's the channel through which people can share their developing necessities, express worries, and proposition support. Ordinary registrations and sincere discussions help to guarantee that the relationship stays lined up with the true selves of those included. Correspondence additionally fills in as the extension over which difficulties are confronted and settled, fortifying the association simultaneously.

The Job of Pardoning and Understanding: False impressions and clashes are normal in any relationship. What decides the flexibility of the relationship is the capacity to move toward such difficulties with absolution and understanding. Perceiving that everybody has their faults, and deciding to gain and develop from these encounters, instead of permitting them to make enduring breaks, is essential. Pardoning, combined with a real work to grasp the other's viewpoint, recuperates and invigorates the security.

Commending the Excursion Together: The excursion of keeping a legitimate relationship is loaded up with snapshots of bliss, challenge, development, and revelation. Commending this excursion — recognizing the achievements came to and the deterrents survive — extends the appreciation for the relationship and for one another. It's tied in with perceiving the excellence in the actual excursion, the common encounters that weave the novel embroidery of your association.

All in all, keeping up with bona fide connections is a continuous excursion of exertion, variation, and responsibility. It's tied in with picking, a large number of days, to sustain the association, to stay transparent, and to become together through the promising and less promising times of life. These connections, based on an underpinning of genuineness, become wellsprings of fantastic strength, euphoria, and satisfaction, enhancing each part of life. Through the ceaseless sustaining of these associations, we track down the excellence of persevering through friendship as well as the significant experience of being known, cherished, and acknowledged for our actual selves.

Praising the Excursion Together: The Craft of Valuing Genuine Connections

In the domain of valid connections, the act of praising the excursion together stands as an essential demonstration of their worth and versatility. This festival isn't just about stamping achievements or accomplishments yet about perceiving the magnificence of the common way itself — the preliminaries explored, the development experienced, and the extending of bonds that happens through the heap snapshots of association. It is an affirmation of the shared exertion and devotion that supports these connections, making them wellsprings of significant euphoria and strength in our lives.

Perceiving Development and Change: Valid connections are dynamic, advancing close by the people inside them. Praising this development implies recognizing the manners by which the two players have developed, adjusted, and changed over the long run. It's tied in with seeing and valuing the individual for who they are turning out to be, similarly as for you. This acknowledgment cultivates a profound feeling of appreciation and regard, supporting the bond and empowering proceeded with development.

Regarding Shared Encounters: Each common giggle, each steady hug, and, surprisingly, every conflict that prompts further comprehension adds to the texture of a valid relationship. Praising these encounters, both the happy and the difficult, underlines their significance in molding the association. It's an approach to saying, "Each second we've shared has esteem and has brought us closer." This mentality transforms even the least difficult communications into loved recollections, constructing a repository of shared delight that can support the relationship during harder times.

Exploring Difficulties with Solidarity: The excursion of a valid relationship perpetually incorporates difficulties. Commending the excursion together includes perceiving the strength and flexibility created by confronting these difficulties joined together. Whether it's beating outside snags or dealing with unseen struggles, each obstacle crossed together is a triumph. Recognizing these triumphs supports the thought that anything what's in store holds, it very well may be explored next to each other.

Making Ceremonies of Appreciation: Laying out customs or customs that honor the relationship can be a strong approach to praising the excursion. These can be pretty much as basic as a yearly day devoted to pondering the year's development and difficulties or as private as a common diary of considerations and encounters. Such customs become hallowed spaces of association, building up the worth put on the relationship and on one another's presence in your lives.

The Nonstop Reestablishment of Responsibility: Commending the excursion of a genuine relationship is, basically, a consistent recharging of obligation to that relationship. All it's a continuous decision to value, regard, and backing each other through life's seasons. This responsibility isn't static however develops and extends with each test and win shared, with each snapshot of weakness and association. It is the comprehension that the excursion together isn't simply a piece of life however a central component of every individual's development and bliss.

In praising the excursion of genuine connections, we recognize the significant effect of these associations on our lives. We honor the work, the adoration, and the strength that supports them, and we focus on proceeding with the excursion with receptiveness, understanding, and bliss. This festival is a sign of the excellence found in evident association and the groundbreaking force of strolling through existence with the people who know and value our real selves. Through this festival, we reinforce our connections as well as confirm the significant job they play in our excursion toward living our best, most genuine lives.

| 6 |

Chapter 6: Living Authentically in a Digital World

Exploring the Advanced Scene with Credibility

In a time where the computerized world is an expansion of our actual reality, residing truly requires cognizant route through virtual spaces. The web, virtual entertainment, and different advanced stages offer exceptional open doors for association, articulation, and learning. Be that as it may, they likewise present remarkable difficulties to keeping up with credibility. This part starts by investigating how we can draw in with the computerized world such that praises our actual selves, encouraging authentic associations and encounters on the web.

The Situation with two sides of Computerized Network: The advanced world is a tremendous breadth of data and connection, where limits between the individual and public frequently obscure. On one hand, it offers the capacity to interface with similar people across the globe, to share our interests, and to openly communicate our characters. On the other, it very well may be a domain of organized personas, where the strain to introduce a glorified rendition of ourselves can diminish our realness.

Developing Advanced Care: To explore the computerized scene with genuineness, we should develop advanced care. This includes being cognizant and conscious by they way we draw in web based, settling on decisions that line up with our qualities and genuine selves. It implies wondering why we are sharing what we share, drawing in with the substance we draw in with, and whether these activities serve our authentic advantages or on the other hand in the event that they're driven by the longing for endorsement or approval.

Genuine Articulation in an Organized World: Communicating our thoughts truly in a computerized world that frequently esteems feature reels over genuine requires fortitude and mindfulness. It's tied in with tracking down the harmony between sharing our lives and saving our protection. Real articulation online means permitting ourselves to be helpless, to share our bits of insight, battles, and wins such that feels veritable to us, without capitulating to the tension of depicting a glorified life.

The Significance of Purposeful Associations: In the advanced domain, the amount of associations can undoubtedly eclipse their quality. Living genuinely online means focusing on deliberate associations over shallow ones. It includes participating in networks and discussions that resound with our true advantages and values, where shared help and authentic association are the underpinnings of the association.

Safeguarding Genuineness In the midst of Computerized Commotion: The consistent flood of data, feelings, and correlations in the advanced world can be overpowering, making it hard to remain grounded in our legitimacy. Safeguarding our bona fide selves online requires defining limits around our computerized utilization and cooperations. This could mean arranging our feeds to mirror our actual advantages, restricting time spent on computerized stages, or taking customary advanced detoxes to reconnect with our internal identities and the actual world around us.

Exploring the computerized scene with legitimacy is a dynamic and continuous cycle. It requires care, deliberateness, and a promise to remaining consistent with ourselves in the midst of the steadily changing computerized flows. By moving toward our advanced commitment with reason and realness, we can make significant associations and encounters that enhance our lives and mirror our actual selves.

Genuine Articulation in an Organized World

In the computerized age, the line among legitimacy and curation obscures, provoking us to explore a mind boggling snare of self-show and veritable articulation. This part digs into the subtleties of keeping up with our bona fide selves in a world that frequently remunerates cleaned personas and feature reels. It's a call to embrace the untidy, unfiltered real factors of our lives and to share our insights in a manner that resounds with our fundamental beliefs, in any event, when it contradicts some common norms of computerized compulsiveness.

The Deception of Flawlessness: Web-based entertainment stages are immersed with pictures and accounts of wonderful lives — perfect appearances, unspoiled encounters, and consistent examples of overcoming adversity. This organized flawlessness can make a distinction, an inclination that our genuine lives, with their intricacies and blemishes, some way or another miss the mark. Genuine articulation in this setting implies recognizing that the facade of flawlessness is only that — a facade — and that genuine is perfectly blemished.

Overcoming Weakness On the web: To check the arranged flawlessness, conquering weakness turns into a demonstration of defiance and genuineness. Sharing our difficulties, disappointments, and vulnerabilities welcomes association and sympathy, advising us that we're in good company in our battles. Nonetheless, this weakness should be explored with care, picking stages and networks where such receptiveness is met with help as opposed to judgment.

Making Spaces for Legitimacy: One of the most enabling activities we can take is to make and encourage advanced spaces that celebrate credibility. This can mean supporting substance that reflects reality, participating in genuine discussions, and contributing our own true voices to the blend. Thusly, we assist with building a computerized culture that values profundity and association over triviality.

The Harmony Among Sharing and Security: True articulation doesn't require sharing everything. Genuine credibility regards the limits among public and confidential life. It's tied in with sharing what feels right to us, what fills our need, and what lines up with our qualities, all while keeping a space that is only as far as we're concerned or for our nearby circle. This equilibrium is critical for guaranteeing that our computerized articulation upgrades as opposed to cheapens our identity.

Embracing Our Diverse Selves: At last, legitimate articulation in the advanced world includes embracing and introducing our multi-layered selves. We are complicated creatures with a scope of feelings, interests, and encounters. Our computerized personas ought to mirror this intricacy, permitting us to appear as our entire selves, in addition to the parts we believe are satisfactory or engaging.

In a world that frequently conflates perceivability with esteem, picking credible articulation is a demonstration of mental fortitude. It's a guarantee to appearing as we really are, in the entirety of our flawed brilliance, and to looking for associations that are established in veritable comprehension and acknowledgment. Thusly, we improve our own lives as well as add to a more true, merciful computerized world.

The Significance of Deliberate Associations

In the immense field of the computerized world, where associations can be made with a basic snap, the genuine embodiment of relationship frequently loses all sense of direction in interpretation. The third foundation of living truly in a computerized age centers around the development of deliberate associations — connections that rise above the triviality of preferences, remarks, and follows, to contact the center of veritable human experience. This quest for profundity over broadness in our computerized connections isn't simply an inclination yet a need for those looking to legitimately live.

Picking Higher expectations when in doubt: The computerized age entices us with the charm of endless associations, yet obvious satisfaction comes from the quality, not the amount, of these connections. Deliberate associations are those that offer genuine benefit and significance, enhancing our lives and encouraging a feeling of local area and having a place. These associations are made with reason and kept up with care, mirroring a common craving for certifiable connection and backing.

Making Significant Advanced Spaces: To encourage purposeful associations, one should be conscious in making and partaking in computerized spaces that line up with one's qualities and interests. This implies searching out networks and gatherings that reverberate on a more profound level, where the trading of thoughts and backing goes past the surface. These spaces become sanctuaries for real articulation and significant commitment, where people can interface over shared interests and weaknesses.

The Job of Dynamic Commitment: Deliberate associations require dynamic commitment. This goes past detached looking to include significant communication — sharing contemplations, clarifying pressing issues, and offering support. It's tied in with being available in our advanced connections, treating them with similar consideration and regard we would face to face experiences. By connecting effectively, we signal our interest in the relationship, supporting an association that can possibly develop and extend after some time.

Exploring the Catch 22 of Computerized Closeness: The advanced world offers a perplexing type of closeness. On one hand, it permits us to share and associate easily, frequently uncovering parts of ourselves we could delay to face to face. On the other, it can make a feeling of distance, a support that causes certifiable weakness to feel more secure. Exploring this conundrum requires care — monitoring how we introduce ourselves on the web and endeavoring to be however genuine and open as we may be fit for being, inside the limits of individual solace and security.

Supporting Associations Over the long haul: Deliberate associations, similar as their disconnected partners, need supporting to maintain and develop. This includes standard registrations, recalling significant subtleties and occasions, and appearing for each other in the midst of hardship. It additionally implies being willing to advance together, perceiving that computerized connections, similar to all connections, can change and foster after some time.

In this present reality where computerized cooperations can frequently feel brief and meager, the quest for deliberate associations remains as a reference point of genuineness. It advises us that behind each screen lies a human heart, looking for figuring out, acknowledgment, and certified association. By deciding to draw in with deliberateness, we improve our own computerized encounters as well as add to a more associated, genuine, and merciful web-based world.

Conclusion: Embracing Your Authentic Journey

Reflection and Development: The Heartbeat of Genuineness

At the center of our excursion toward carrying on with a bona fide life lies the constant course of reflection and development. This excursion, innately private yet all around thunderous, provokes us to dive into the profundities of what our identity is, to address, to tune in, and to advance. A way requests we focus on the illustrations life offers us, both in snapshots of euphoria and in preliminaries, understanding that each experience holds the possibility to shape our genuine selves.

The Reflection of Reflection: Reflection is the mirror through which we view the shapes of our lives, inspecting our convictions, values, and activities. It includes searching internally with trustworthiness and mental fortitude, finding out if our outer lives mirror our actual internal identities. This course of reflection can be both testing and freeing, as it expects us to go up against parts of ourselves we might have overlooked or covered. However, it is in this a conflict that we track down the chance for genuine development.

The Way of Development: Development, then, at that point, is the regular movement from reflection — a dynamic and some of the time awkward course of extending past our ongoing limits. It includes shedding obsolete convictions, embracing new information, and venturing into the obscure with transparency and interest. Development isn't straight; it's a twisting of realizing, where each cycle carries us nearer to our center selves, outfitted with more profound comprehension and strength.

Gaining from Life's Educational program: Life, in a display of divine insight, offers an educational program rich with potential open doors for development. Every relationship, challenge, achievement, and misfortune is an illustration in mask, provoking us to extend our viewpoints and to develop a more profound identity mindfulness. Embracing life's examples requires a readiness to be powerless, to scrutinize the natural, and to confide during the time spent becoming.

The Job of Care: Care is a priceless buddy on the excursion of reflection and development. It secures us right now, permitting us to notice our contemplations, sentiments, and responses without judgment. Through care, we develop a merciful mindfulness that directs our appearance, enlightens our development ways, and assists us with exploring the intricacies of living legitimately.

A Guarantee to Persistent Development: Eventually, embracing reflection and development is a promise to nonstop development. It's an affirmation that we are works underway, consistently on the way of turning out to be all the more profoundly ourselves. This excursion doesn't have a last objective; rather, it offers waypoints of figuring out, epiphanies, and achievements of change. Each step taken in realness carries us nearer to our actual selves as well as enhances our commitment with our general surroundings.

In embracing our true process, we focus on a long lasting course of reflection and development. This responsibility provokes us to live with expectation, to embrace our weaknesses, and to commend our developing selves. It is through this persistent interaction that we open our actual potential and carry on with our best lives, set apart by profundity, meaning, and certifiable self-articulation.

Fortitude to Be Valid

In the embroidered artwork of life, fortitude is the string that winds through the core of our real process. The power drives us forward, encouraging us to embrace our actual selves in a world that frequently esteems congruity over uniqueness. This section commends the boldness expected to stand firm in one's reality, to voice one's exceptional points of view, and to live as per one's most profound qualities and convictions, in any event, when it implies remaining solitary.

The Quintessence of Mental fortitude: Boldness with regards to legitimacy isn't about the shortfall of dread. Rather, it's tied in with recognizing our apprehensions — of dismissal, judgment, or disappointment — and deciding to push ahead notwithstanding them. The internal strength permits us to uncover who we genuinely are, to share our contemplations, convictions, and dreams with the world, in any event, when we risk analysis or misconception.

Confronting Cultural Tensions: The excursion towards genuineness is frequently met with obstruction, from inside as well as from the general public around us. Normal practices and assumptions can apply a strong impact, empowering us to fit in as opposed to stick out. The fortitude to be consistent with oneself, then, is likewise a boldness to oppose these tensions, to scrutinize the norm, and to cut out a space where one's actual self can thrive.

The Gamble of Weakness: At the core of validness lies weakness — the eagerness to be viewed as we are, with every one of our defects and vulnerabilities. Embracing weakness requires massive mental fortitude. It includes freeing ourselves up to likely harmed and dismissal, however it likewise permits us to interface profoundly with others, to cherish and be adored really, and to carry on with an existence of extravagance and profundity.

The Prize of Living Genuinely: The fortitude to be consistent with oneself accompanies significant prizes. It frees us from the heaviness of misrepresentation and the weariness of attempting to be somebody else. It prompts an existence of honesty, where our activities line up with our qualities, and our connections are based on real association. This realness brings a feeling of harmony and satisfaction that can't be tracked down in living differently.

Supporting Boldness Inside: Developing the mental fortitude to live genuinely is an everyday practice. It starts with little advances — shouting out about a minor bad form, communicating an individual inclination, or sharing a piece of our actual selves with somebody we trust. Over the long haul, these little demonstrations of valiance expand upon one another, reinforcing our mental fortitude muscle and engaging us to pursue bolder decisions in arrangement with our credible selves.

In embracing the boldness to be valid, we honor our own process as well as light the way for others to follow. We become reference points of plausibility, showing that a daily existence lived truly isn't just feasible however profoundly fulfilling. As we push ahead, let us convey this fortitude as a light, enlightening our way and motivating others to set out on their own excursion of credibility.

The Force of Weakness

At the center of our legitimate excursion lies the force of weakness, an idea that is both overwhelming and freeing. To be helpless is to free ourselves up to the chance of harmed, yet it is additionally to open the way to certified association, profound comprehension, and significant self-improvement. This section dives into the strength that can be found in weakness, testing the misinterpretation that it is a shortcoming, and commending it as a foundation of living legitimately.

Rethinking Weakness: Weakness is many times misconstrued as an indication of shortcoming, a defect to be stowed away. However, at its pith, weakness is a demonstration of boldness. It is the eagerness to appear and be seen, to share our actual selves, including our apprehensions, dreams, and instabilities, without knowing the result. This redefinition moves our point of view, permitting us to see weakness not as a responsibility but rather as a way to credibility.

The Doorway to Association: The force of weakness lies in capacity to produce associations rise above the shallow. At the point when we share our actual selves with others, we welcome them to do likewise, making a space where veritable connections can thrive. This shared weakness cultivates a feeling of having a place and understanding, components that are vital for close to home prosperity and which can't flourish in that frame of mind of misrepresentation.

Embracing Our Blemishes: A piece of weakness is tolerating our flaws and daring to impart them to the world. This acknowledgment is freeing. It liberates us from the debilitating quest for flawlessness and permits us to embrace our mankind. At the point when we are open about our defects, we observe that they are not boundaries to association but rather spans, shared parts of the human experience that attract us nearer to other people.

Weakness as a Wellspring of Solidarity: The eagerness to be helpless likewise fills in as a strong wellspring of solidarity. It requires internal flexibility to confront expected judgment or dismissal and to keep remaining in our reality. This versatility works over the long run, enabling us to explore life's difficulties with beauty and genuineness. Besides, by embracing weakness, we move others to do likewise, making a gradually expanding influence that can change connections and networks.

The Excursion Towards Embracing Weakness: Figuring out how to embrace weakness is a slow interaction, one that includes contemplation, practice, and persistence. It begins with little demonstrations of transparency, sharing an individual story, offering a disliked viewpoint, or conceding we don't have every one of the responses. Each step in the right direction supports that being defenseless isn't only protected yet fundamental for living a full, true life.

In perceiving the force of weakness, we recognize that our most noteworthy strength lies in our capacity to be completely human, imperfections and everything. This section welcomes us to shed the defensive layer we've worked around our souls, to appear on the planet as we genuinely are, and to interface with others on a degree of profound, credible human experience. In doing as such, we enhance our own lives as well as add to a more open, understanding, and humane world.

Local area and Association

As we venture towards living legitimately, we find that while the way is profoundly private, it need not be crossed in isolation. This section dives into the crucial job of local area and association as we continued looking for genuineness, featuring how the help, understanding, and reverberation of similar people can fundamentally advance and enable our excursion.

The Quintessence of Local area: Local area offers a mirror to our bona fide selves, reflecting back the legitimacy and worth of our internal bits of insight. In spaces where our actual selves are invited and celebrated, we track down the fortitude to completely investigate and communicate our characters more. These people group — whether fashioned in actual spaces or developed in the computerized world — give a feeling of having a place that is fundamental for our close to home and mental prosperity.

Tracking down Your Clan: The mission for credibility frequently drives us to search out those with comparable qualities, battles, and goals. Tracking down your clan — a gathering of people who acknowledge as well as love your actual self — can be an extraordinary encounter. Inside these circles, we are conceded the opportunity to be defenseless, to share our fantasies and questions, and to help each other in our particular processes. This common trade cultivates a profound feeling of association and having a place that strengthens us against the difficulties of the rest of the world.

The Force of Shared Encounters: One of the most significant parts of local area is the sharing of encounters. Through stories, we understand we are in good company in our battles or one of a kind in our longings. This common story can be amazingly approving, offering solace and consolation. Besides, seeing the excursion of others gives a wellspring of motivation and picking up, offering bits of knowledge and techniques that we can apply to our own way.

Adding to the Local area: While getting backing and understanding from a local area is priceless, similarly significant is our commitment to it. By offering our own encounters, experiences, and support, we help to establish a sustaining climate for other people. This correspondence reinforces the texture of the local area, guaranteeing it stays a dynamic and strong space for every one of its individuals. In giving, we likewise get — an update that our battles and victories can act as a guide for other people.

The Far reaching influence of Legitimate Associations: Genuine associations inside a local area have a far reaching influence, stretching out past the quick circle to impact the more extensive society. As we epitomize realness in our collaborations, we rouse others to investigate their actual selves, encouraging a culture that qualities and praises uniqueness and variety. This aggregate shift towards legitimacy has the ability to change cultural standards, empowering a more open, tolerating, and veritable world.

Taking everything into account, local area and association are essential to our real process. They offer the help, motivation, and feeling of having a place that fuel our proceeded with development and self-investigation. As we produce these credible associations, we improve our own lives as well as add to the production of a more real, associated world. Through the force of local area, we are reminded that while the excursion to legitimacy is our own, we are undeniably associated in our common human experience.

Embracing Change: The Liquid Idea of Credibility

In the finishing up part of our investigation into living genuinely, we direct our concentration toward the dynamic and advancing scene of our actual selves. Embracing change isn't only an idea however a key part of genuineness. It recognizes that as we venture through life, our encounters, connections, and self-awareness consistently shape and re-classify what our identity is. This acknowledgment welcomes us to hold our characters with open hands, prepared to find and incorporate new features of our being.

The Certainty of Progress: Change is a steady friend on the excursion of life. It appears through our advancing contemplations, sentiments, convictions, and connections. Perceiving this, realness requests an adaptability of self — an eagerness to address recently held bits of insight and to adjust even with new encounters. This receptiveness to change doesn't imply precariousness yet rather a profound obligation to self-awareness and self-disclosure.

Development Through Life's Seasons: As we explore the different times of our lives, from the difficulties we face to the achievements we commend, each experience adds to our advancing identity. Embracing change implies seeing these encounters as any open doors for development, permitting them to grow how we might interpret what our identity is and who we seek to be. It includes praising our triumphs,

gaining from our difficulties, and tracking down esteem in each snapshot of the excursion.

The Valid Self as a Work Underway: Survey ourselves as works in
progress can free us from the strain to have everything sorted out. It
urges us to move toward existence with interest, to explore different
avenues regarding better approaches for being, and to embrace the
obscure with certainty. This point of view encourages a strength that is
established in the information that we are continually developing, consistently turning out to be more lined up with our legitimate selves.

Exploring Character and Change: The most common way of
embracing change is innately private and can differ extraordinarily
starting with one individual then onto the next. It requires a sharp
mindfulness and a devotion to thoughtfulness, permitting us to observe
which changes mirror our actual selves and which are responses to
outer tensions. This acumen is essential, as it empowers us to pursue
decisions that truly reverberate with our center being.

The Mental fortitude to Stay Open: At last, embracing change is a
demonstration of boldness. It expects us to stay open to the likelihood
that what our identity is today may not be who we will be tomorrow.
However, in this receptiveness, we track down our actual strength
and the substance of credibility. By inviting change, we certify our
obligation to carrying on with a day to day existence that is consistent
with ourselves, one that praises our past, commends our present, and
anticipates our future with trust and interest.

As we finish up this excursion, let us embrace the liquid idea of
credibility, perceiving that our actual selves are not fixed focuses but
rather gorgeous, advancing articulations of life. In doing as such, we
focus on a long lasting excursion of disclosure, development, and veritable self-articulation, directed by the consistently changing scene of
our souls and brains.